W9-AXO-582

PET CARE GUIDES FOR KIDS

KITTEN

Mark Evans

DK

A DK PUBLISHING BOOK

For Mum and Dad

Project Editor Liza Bruml
Art Editor Jane Coney
Editor Miriam Farbey
Designer Rebecca Johns
U.S. Editor B. Alison Weir
Photographer Paul Bricknell
Illustrators Sally Hynard and Peter Visscher
ASPCA Consultant Stephen Zawistowski, Ph.D.

First American Edition, 1992
6 8 10 9 7

Published in the United Stated by
DK Publishing, Inc., Madison Avenue
New York, New York 10016

Copyright © 1992 Dorling Kindersley Limited, London
Text copyright © 1992 Mark Evans
Foreword © 1992 Roger Caras

Visit us on the Wold Wide Web at
http://www.dk.com

All rights reserved under International and Pan-American
Copyright Conventions. No part of this publication may
be reproduced, stored in a retrieval system, or transmitted
in any form or by any means, electronic, mechanical,
photocopying, recording, or otherwise, without the
prior written permission of the copyright owner.
Published in Great Britain by Dorling Kindersley Limited.

Library of Congress Cataloging-in-Publication Data
Evans, Mark.
    Kitten / Mark Evans. — 1st American ed.
    p. cm. — (ASPCA pet care guides for kids)
    Includes index.
    Summary: Describes different kinds of cats and discusses how to
select and care for one.
    ISBN 1-56458-126-8
    1. Cats—Juvenile literature. 2. Kittens—Juvenile literature.
[1. Cats. 2. Pets.] I. Title. II. Series.
SF445.7.E82 1992   92-52827
636.8'07—dc20   CIP
                                                        AC

Color reproduction by Colourscan, Singapore
Printed and bound in Spain by Artes Gráficas Toledo, S.A.
D.L.TO: 1826-1997

Models: Narada Bernard, Jacob Brubert, Martin Cooles, Louisa Hall,
Corinne Hogarth, Thanh Huynh, Gupreet Janday, Jason Kerim,
Nathalie Lyon, Rachel Mamauag, Paul Mitchell, Florence Prowen,
Isabel Prowen, Jamie Sallon, Maia Terry, Lisa Wardropper

Dorling Kindersley would like to thank everyone who allowed us to
photograph their pet, Jane Burton and Wood Green Animal Shelters for
providing cats, Christopher Howson for design help, Bridget
Hopkinson and Louise Pritchard for editorial help, and Lynn Bresler
for the index.

Picture credits: Jane Burton p28 b, p29 cr, p35 cr, p40 tr, b, p41 tl, cl,
bl, br; Dave King p17 bc; NHPA/Stephen Dalton p12 tr;
NHPA/Manfred Danegger p13 tl; NHPA/Gerard Lacz p16 tc,
p17 br; Steve Shott p34 tr

Foreword

Kittens are among the Earth's greatest treasures. When your kitten arrives, you must not mistake it for a stuffed toy. It feels pain, and it can be afraid, just as you can. Be quiet around your kitten, don't confuse it. Your kitten will soon become a cat, but its needs will be the same: nourishment, security, love, and very good veterinary care. Have fun, and know that being a good, responsible animal owner is one of the nicest things that you can be!

Roger Caras
ASPCA President

Note to parents

This book teaches your child how to be a caring and responsible pet owner. But remember, your child must have your help and guidance in every aspect of day-to-day pet care. Don't let your child have a cat unless you are sure that your family has the time and resources to care for it properly—for the whole of its life.

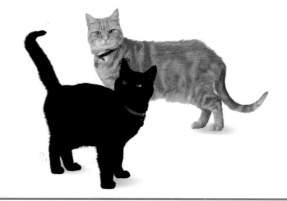

Contents

Introduction

The first step to becoming a good cat owner is to choose the right sort of cat. It is how a cat behaves that is most important, not what she looks like or how old she is. She is going to be your best friend. You will spend a lot of time playing together. But remember, you need to care for her every day. Not just to start with, but for the whole of her life.

You will need to buy special things for your cat

Understanding your pet
By watching your cat carefully, you will learn her special way of talking. From a flick of her tail to the movement of her ears, you will see if she is happy or sad. And you will soon understand what she is saying when she meows or purrs.

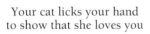
Your cat licks your hand to show that she loves you

Caring for your pet
You will be your cat's best friend only if you care for her properly. You will need to make sure that she eats the right foods, always has water, and can get plenty of exercise every day. You will also have to groom her often, and spend some time training her.

You will need to groom your cat every day

Things to do with your pet

Your cat loves to play with toys. She likes chasing and pouncing games the best. These help her practice her hunting skills.

Your kitten will bat a dangling toy

People to help

The best cat owner always tries to find out more about her pet. You can ask your veterinarian any questions you have about how to keep your pet healthy.

You will need to visit your veterinarian regularly

New family member

Your cat is a very independent animal. But if you care for her properly, she will enjoy being part of your family. She can even make a good friend for some of your other pets. You can train her to obey the rules you and your family make for her.

Things to remember:
When you live with a pet cat, there are some important rules you must always follow:

🐾 Wash your hands after petting or playing with your cat.

🐾 Never allow your cat to eat food from your plate.

🐾 Don't let your cat on the kitchen counters or the dinner table.

🐾 Don't let your cat on your bed.

🐾 If your cat is fast asleep, don't wake her up suddenly.

🐾 Never, ever tease or hit your cat.

Ask a grown-up
👫 When you see this sign in the book, you should ask an adult to help you.

Your cat will become part of your family

What is a cat?

Cats belong to a group of animals called mammals. Like all mammals, cats have warm blood and a furry body. When they are young, they drink milk from their mothers. Not all cats look the same. They can be big or small, long-haired or short-haired. As they grow up, they develop keen senses and supple, athletic bodies.

Ear can turn in every direction to pick up sounds

Narrow shoulders allow cat to slip through small spaces

Life on four legs

Every part of your cat's body does its own job. His fur coat keeps him warm. His slender body lets him squeeze through tiny gaps and twist around obstacles. Strong muscles power his hind legs so he can jump a long way and run fast over short distances. His long tail helps him balance.

Thick fur helps keep cat warm

Pink nipple

Rough, pink paw pads give good grip

Flat belly button is hidden by fur

Claws are kept in a skin pocket called a sheath

Underneath your cat

Look closely at your cat's belly and you will find that she has a flat belly button. Female cats usually have eight nipples. In a mother cat, they are sucked for milk by her young kittens.

Ear perks
up to listen

Pupil becomes
small slit in
bright light

Moist nose
detects smells

Whiskers feel in
the dark to help
him find his way

Long tail swings
from side to side
for balance

Super senses

Your cat has better senses than humans. He sees
more clearly than you in dim light. He hears
faint sounds when you think it is quiet. He
can even tell if other cats have been around
by sniffing for their special scents.

Upright
tail shows
cat is alert

Heel is a long way
off the ground—this
helps him run faster

Four-toed
back paw has
sharp claws

Back leg is large
and strong

He always
stands on tiptoes

Look closer
at your cat

Pointed teeth, called
canines, are used
to hold food.

Black pupils change
shape depending on
the amount of light.

Hooklike front claws
come out of sheaths
for grasping.

Five-toed front paws
have rough pads for
protection.

Tiny spines on
tongue strip meat off
bones and pick out
dirt from fur.

Life in the wild

Domestic cats are members of the felid family. Wild members of this family include big cats such as tigers, and small cats, like lynxes. Wild cats usually live on their own. A very long time ago, small wild cats began to kill the mice and rats that ate people's grain. The people cared for the most friendly cats and they soon became pets.

European wild cat

Always wild

The European wild cat, like many small wild cats, is very shy. Even though it looks like a domestic cat, it is so timid that it can never live with people. But the North African wild cat is bolder. It is thought to be the ancestor of the domestic cat.

This feral long-haired cat has dirty, matted fur

Brave cat crouches, ready to pounce

Cat sits and watches all the other cats

Tough cat stares

Old cat lies down but keeps a sharp lookout

Lioness stays close to the young cubs

Pride of lions

Some big cats, such as lions, live together in a family group, called a pride. There may be as many as 20 lions in a pride. Together, they hunt and kill wild animals for food.

Your parents will help you decide the rules for your cat

Alley cats

Domestic cats that live wild in cities and on farms are called feral cats. They often live in groups. They hunt small animals for food and eat waste scraps. When there is not enough food, some cats leave the group. The cats that stay together may fight over food.

Kitten looks for someone to play with

Alert cat has tail in the air

New friends

People make good friends for cats. You feed them, give them a warm place to sleep, and keep their coats neat and clean. Although most cats are independent, they will enjoy being part of the family if you care for them properly.

Cat lies down to sleep while others keep watch

Types of cats

Many years ago, some people began to breed many special-looking types of cats. They chose cats with unusual features, such as long hair, or beautiful coat colors. Many types, or breeds, of cats with different looks were produced. Some cats are a mixture of breeds.

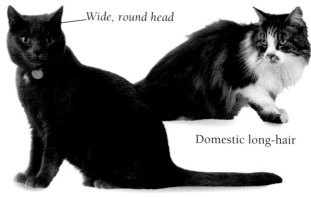

Wide, round head

Domestic long-hair

Domestic short-hair

Domestic cats
The most common type of cat is called a domestic. All domestics are crossbreds. Domestics have large, broad heads. Some have long hair, others have short, sleek coats.

Siamese
Siamese cats have short fur, a lean body, and a pointed head. They are very friendly and meow very often.

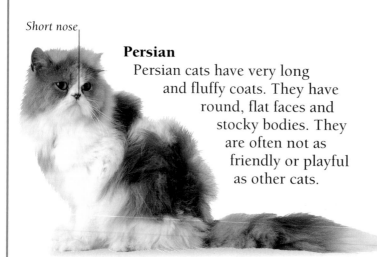

Large, pointed ears

Smooth, sleek coat

Siamese

Fine coat dries quickly

Turkish Van

Turkish Van
Turkish Van cats have very silky coats. Unlike other cats, they love to play in water. They are often called Turkish swimming cats.

Short nose

Persian
Persian cats have very long and fluffy coats. They have round, flat faces and stocky bodies. They are often not as friendly or playful as other cats.

Persian

Dark brown diamond patch on face

Ragdoll

Fur is thick and silky

Coat is sleek and glossy

Burmese

Purebreds and mixed breeds

Two purebreds have another purebred.

Purebred looks just like its parents.

Maine Coon

Ragdoll
Large and gentle Ragdoll cats look like Birmans. But if you pick them up, they will hang limply—like ragdolls!

Maine Coon
Big, strong Maine Coon cats have shaggy coats. They make loving pets.

Burmese
Although closely related to Siamese cats, Burmese cats have rounder faces. They are very active and love people.

Birman
Lively Birman cats enjoy company. They may look like Siameses, but they have longer coats.

Birman

Long and fluffy tail

Different purebreds have a crossbred.

A crossbred is a mixture of its parents.

Fur is very long on chest and belly

Abyssinian
Beautiful Abyssinians are very slender, with long, thin legs and big ears. They are alert and clever, and often make a lot of noise.

Short, dense fur

Two crossbreds have a mixed breed cat.

Abyssinian mother and kittens

Every mixed breed cat looks slightly different.

Selecting for looks

All cats have the same parts—a head with eyes, ears, mouth, and nose, and a body with a furry coat. The size, shape, and color of these parts is different in every cat. But don't be tempted to choose a cat just for her looks. Look at the way she behaves as well. After all, you are choosing a friend for life.

Scottish Fold

Domestic short-hair

Burmese

Maine Coon

Domestic short-hair

Persian

Head shapes

Most cats have a round head with a wide face. Persian cats have a broad head and a very flat face. Other cats have a narrow head with a pointed face.

Tonkinese

Big or small ears?

Cats can have all kinds of ears. Most mixed breed cats have small, pointed ears. Cats that first came from hot countries often have large ears. Some cats have hairy ears, while other cats' ears are even folded!

Coat colors

A cat's coat may be all one color, such as black, white, or brown. Some coats are a mixture of two or more colors. When a cat is orangey-tan and black, it is called a tortoiseshell.

Tortoiseshell tail

White back

Black fur

Black back

White leg

Bi-colored coat

Tri-colored coat

Plain coat

Coat patterns

Cats may have a spotted pattern all over their coats. Other cats, called tabby, have a striped coat. Many cats have blotchy coats. When dark patches are on the ears, face, paws, and tail, they are called "points."

Dark spots ring tail

Black spots

"Points" on ears

Tabby pattern on back with white patch

Ocicat

Dark tail

Siamese

Brown paws

White paws

Domestic short-hair

Long hair is soft

Short coat is smooth

Ragdoll

Domestic tabby and white

Hairstyles for cats

Fur can be many different lengths. Most domestic cats have short hair. It is easy to clean, and it does not get knotted. Long-haired cats have silky coats that can tangle. Their fur must be brushed every day.

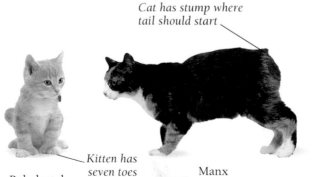

No whiskers

Hairless skin is wrinkly

Cat has stump where tail should start

Extraordinary and strange

Some cats have very unusual features. Manx cats look like ordinary cats, but have no tails! Polydactyl cats are born with too many toes. Instead of five on each front paw, they have as many as seven. Another unusual cat is the almost furless Sphynx.

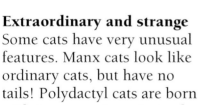

Kitten has seven toes

Polydactyl

Manx

Sphynx

Getting ready

You will need to get some special equipment for your new pet. All the items should be well made. Make sure everything is ready before you pick up your kitten. Put away dangerous things because kittens will try to play with almost anything.

Wire cage

Plastic carrying box

Carrying baskets
You need a basket in which to carry your kitten. Ask your veterinarian for a special carrying box, or a strong wire cage.

Litter tray

Plastic garbage bin

Soil

Wood pellets

Clay

Cozy bed
Your kitten will sleep in all sorts of places. She will also like to curl up in her soft, warm cat bed.

Covered bed

Feeding equipment
Buy a water bowl, a food bowl, and a plastic container in which to store dried food. To serve the food, get your cat her own spoon and fork.

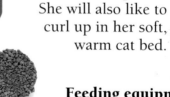
Paper   Litter tray liners   Scoop   Shovel

Airtight container

Spoon

Fork

Water bowl

Food bowl

Litter tray and litter
Cats and kittens that live indoors go to the bathroom in a litter tray. Buy a plastic litter tray and litter liners. You will need some litter, a scoop to fill the tray, and a shovel to clean and empty it. You can keep litter fresh in a storage bin. Find some old paper to put under the tray to keep the floor clean.

Nylon collar

Metal identity tag

Collar

Buy a collar with elastic in it. If the collar gets caught, the elastic will stretch. Your cat can pull her head through to escape.

Metal identity tag

Comb

Brush

Towel

Gooming equipment

Buy your cat a fine comb and a soft brush. Your cat should also have her own towel for you to dry her with.

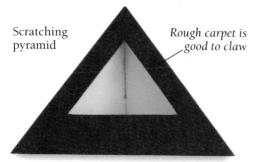

Scratching pyramid

Rough carpet is good to claw

Scratching pyramid

Your cat will want to scratch with her claws. Buy or make a scratching post so she doesn't scratch the furniture.

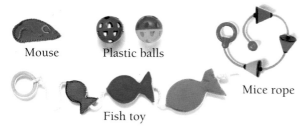

Mouse

Plastic balls

Mice rope

Fish toy

Cat toys

Cats love to play with things that move or make a noise. Buy or make some strong, small toys for your cat.

Identity tag

👫Buy an identity tag to attach to your cat's collar. Have your address and phone number engraved on it.

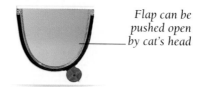

Flap can be pushed open by cat's head

Cat-flap

Your cat likes to get in and out of your house whenever she wants. You might buy a clear cat-flap to put in your door.

Bucket

Rubber gloves

Scrubbing brush

Disinfectant

Odor remover

Squeaky clean

Your cat will sometimes make a mess. You will need some special cleaning things to clean up after her. Always wear your rubber gloves when cleaning.

Danger!

These things can hurt cats:

Trailing cables are dangerous.

Yarn and needles can be swallowed.

Some indoor and garden plants are poisonous.

Cleaning fluids and chemicals harm your cat.

Cats like warm places, but hot things can burn.

Garbage may choke your cat.

19

Choosing your cat

You can choose a kitten from a litter when she is around four weeks old. You can't take her home until she is six weeks old, and ready to leave her mother. Meet the mother cat, so you can see what your kitten will be like when she is fully grown. Make sure the kitten is healthy.

Kitten watches dangling toy

Cuddly kitten
Before you get an adorable kitten, think carefully. You will be kept very busy playing with him and keeping him out of trouble.

Old and wise
You can adopt a grown-up cat that is as friendly as a kitten.

Where to find your new pet
- An animal shelter has cats of all ages and kinds that need new homes.
- A friend's cat may have a litter.
- A breeder will sell you a purebred.

Curious kitten

Noisy kitten

Shy kitten

1 **When the owner takes you** to see the litter, watch from a place where the kittens can't see you. Look for a lively kitten that likes to play with her sisters and brothers. Avoid a kitten that seems like a bully.

2 **Say hello** to the kittens' mother. See if she is friendly. She should start to purr when you stroke her.

Pet the mother cat

Kitten stays close to her mother

3 **Watch the kittens** to see which one is the friendliest. They will think you are a jungle gym and clamber all over you. Pick out the one you like.

Kitten cuddles up to you

4 **Ask the owner** how to pick up your favorite kitten. Find out what sex it is. See if the kitten is healthy. She must have bright eyes and a clean nose. Her mouth should be pale pink, with tiny, white teeth. Check that her coat is clean all over, even under her tail.

Check that each ear is clean

Hold up the kitten to have a good look

Paperwork
Write down the food, medicines, and inoculations your cat has been given. Your veterinarian will want to know.

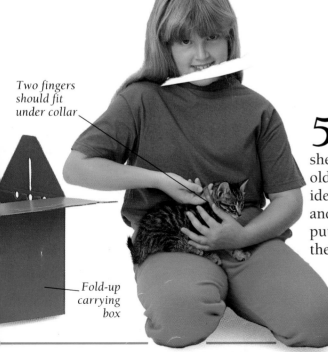

Two fingers should fit under collar

Fold-up carrying box

5 **Go back to pick up** your kitten when she is at least six weeks old. Take the collar and identity tag with you, and a carrying box to put your kitten in on the trip home.

🐾**Boy or girl?**
Male cats are usually bigger than females. They wander farther from home and may get into more fights. You should get your cat neutered when he or she is about six months old (see p. 40).

Welcome home

To help your kitten settle in quickly, get everything ready before she arrives. Put her in one room for the first few days. Make sure that all the windows are shut. After this, she may explore the whole house. She must always be able to get to her bed.

Female cat

Male cat

Visiting your veterinarian
Arrange to visit your veterinarian on the way home from picking up your new kitten. The veterinarian will check your pet all over to make sure she is healthy. He will also tell you if she needs any inoculations.

What sex is your kitten?
When a kitten is very young, it can be hard to tell if it is a male or a female. Ask your veterinarian to check the sex.

How to pick up your kitten
You will want to pick up your kitten to cuddle her or to stop her from getting into trouble! Put one hand under her back legs. Put the other hand around her belly and then lift her. If she starts to wriggle, put her gently down again.

Put one hand gently around her chest

Put one hand under her back legs

Meeting a dog

Your cat and your dog can become best friends. Let them meet as soon as your cat has settled in. Watch them carefully to make sure they don't fight.

Sniffing the new family member

Cat stares at dog

Kitten turns away—he is timid

Cat stares at stranger

Meeting another cat

If you already have one cat, let your new pet get to know it slowly. Don't leave the cats alone together. If your kitten is too playful, the other cat may swipe at him.

Preparing the litter tray

Put the filled litter tray in a quiet corner of the room. Your kitten does not like to eat or sleep near her "bathroom."

Storage bin full of litter

Fill the litter tray

A cozy corner

Choose a warm corner of the room for your kitten's bed and eating area. Always put down a bowl of water for your kitten. You can also leave her some dry food (see p. 24).

Dangle rope toy for kitten to bat

Cover over bed makes kitten feel safe

Warm bed

(see p. 24).

23

Feeding your cat

Your cat is a carnivore, or meat-eater, but she may eat small amounts of plants and vegetables, too. To keep your cat healthy, only buy food specially made for cats. You can choose between moist or dry food. Ask your veterinarian to help you choose the right food for your cat.

The carnivore
Because your cat needs more protein than a dog, do not buy dog food for your cat.

Your cat eats crouching down

Dry food

Moist food

Side teeth shear
Your cat's razor-sharp side teeth chop food up into pieces small enough to swallow.

All-in-one
The simplest way to feed your cat is with a "complete" food. It contains all the things he needs. The food is either moist or dry. Cats love to crunch dry food.

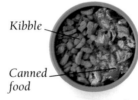

Kibble

Canned food

"Mixed" food

Mixing foods
Your cat may like to try different kinds of foods.

Look for the word "cat"

Buying the food
Carefully read the writing on the packet. Make sure that the food is for cats, and contains meat. This label is from a food for adult cats. A kitten needs a food for growing cats.

CAT FOOD

Fully tested

Food is for cats over one year old. It is a complete pet food.

Feed as much food as your cat will eat in at least two meals a day.

Ingredients: meat and fats
Protein ~%, Oil ~%, Fiber ~%, Water ~%, Vitamins A, D, E
Always leave fresh water.

Best before ~~

~ grams

Look for the word "tested"

Recycling sign

Use by date

Weight

Bar code

Fresh water daily

Your cat must always have a bowl of clean water to drink.

Milk can make your cat sick.

How much to feed

The label tells you how much to feed your cat. Most cats are sensible—they will only eat what they need. If your cat starts to get chubby, give her less food.

Crunchy shapes *Fish-shaped snacks*

Your leftovers may give your cat an upset stomach.

Time for a treat

Only give your cat a few treats each day. If she begs you for treats, do not give her any.

Feeding times

Feed your cat as much as it will eat twice a day. Most cats eat only when they need to. Once opened, canned food will go stale quickly. Clear away any leftover food that hasn't been eaten after half an hour.

Chocolate is bad for your cat.

Bones will choke your cat.

Kitten walks toward smell of food

Put the bowl near your kitten's bed

25

The happy cat

A pet cat can tell you in a lot of ways that he is happy. He doesn't smile and laugh, or talk to you by using words. Instead, he makes a few different noises. Listen carefully, and you will often hear him purring or chirping. He also does certain things to show you that he is content. You will see him playing and sleeping, and feel him brushing against you. You will soon learn to recognize a happy cat.

Cat licks paw to wipe his face

Grooming when relaxed
Your cat may wash himself when he is content, even if he is clean. Sometimes he grooms himself if he is worried, to calm himself down.

The head rub
Your cat's way of greeting you is to rub against you. This is his own way of saying hello. Your cat tries to get as close to you as possible.

Tail up shows cat is interested

Head brushes against your sleeve to give a "head rub"

Cat hears a noise and looks around

Sleepy cat lies down

Cat-napping
When cats are completely relaxed, they will become sleepy. They half-shut their eyes. If something disturbs them, they will get up and have a look.

Marking a friend

If a cat likes you, she makes sure that she will recognize you next time you meet. She rubs her body against you and curls her tail around your legs to mark you with her invisible scent.

Cat wraps herself around your legs to leave her scent

Happy cat wrestles with his favorite toy

Purring with pleasure

You can tell that your cat is happy when you see him play. You will sometimes hear him make a rumbling sound, or purr, when he is content.

Your lap is a comfortable, warm seat

Rough tongue tickles

Cat talk

You will hear when your cat is pleased. She may purr, chirp, or meow. Try to figure out what she is trying to say to you.

Happy meow

Siamese cat is pleased

Sitting comfortably

On your lap, your cat may lick you to wash your skin. He may also push his claws into your legs. He doesn't mean to hurt you—he's saying that he loves you.

The frightened cat

Your cat may sometimes be afraid. If something frightens him he may run and hide. He doesn't like to fight. If another cat tries to come into his territory, he pretends that he is brave. He puffs himself up very large, using every part of his body to say "go away!" If the enemy doesn't leave, your cat may get angry. He may roll over and show his claws and teeth. You will hear him hiss.

What frightens your cat?

Firecrackers terrify cats.

Strange dogs may threaten your cat.

Traveling scares some cats.

Trying to look brave

Sometimes you will see your cat look very different. All his fur stands on end, and his back arches. The pupils in his eyes change from slits to circles. Your cat is scared. He is making himself as large as he can to frighten away whatever is scaring him.

Calming down your cat
- Take away the scary thing.
- Switch off the lights.
- Talk in a soothing voice.
- Give your cat some food.

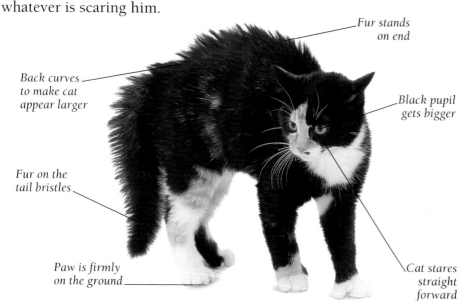

Fur stands on end

Back curves to make cat appear larger

Black pupil gets bigger

Fur on the tail bristles

Paw is firmly on the ground

Cat stares straight forward

Escaping from danger

Cats usually like to run away when they are upset. Your cat may crawl under your bed, or jump up onto a shelf. He likes to sit and watch from a high place where nothing can reach him.

Cat has fled to safety on top shelf

Growling in anger

When your cat is not scared, but very annoyed, she crouches down. She makes a low, grumbling sound, and stares at whatever is upsetting her without blinking. The dark pupils in her eyes become slits. It is best to leave your cat alone when she is irritated.

Pupil is wide slit

Fur is ruffled

Mouth is shut tight

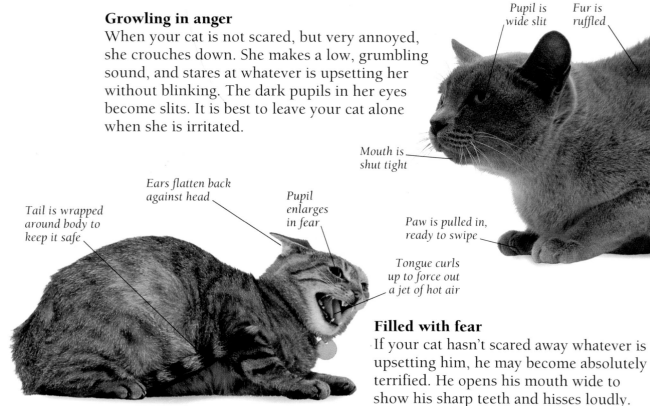

Ears flatten back against head

Pupil enlarges in fear

Tail is wrapped around body to keep it safe

Paw is pulled in, ready to swipe

Tongue curls up to force out a jet of hot air

Filled with fear

If your cat hasn't scared away whatever is upsetting him, he may become absolutely terrified. He opens his mouth wide to show his sharp teeth and hisses loudly.

Training your cat

It is much more difficult to train your cat to sit or stay like a dog. But you can teach her things like her name, where to go to the bathroom, and how to use a cat-flap. And she may surprise you with the things that she teaches herself to do.

Mother cat using her litter tray

Kittens watch their mother

Learning from mother
Young kittens watch their mother go to the bathroom in a litter tray. They quickly learn that when they want to go, they should also use the tray.

Litter training your pet
Every half an hour, when your kitten is awake, gently lift him into the tray. Your kitten will prefer to have his tray in a quiet corner of the room, away from his food.

Carefully lift your kitten into his litter tray

Tray filled with fresh litter

Litter liner

Keeping the tray clean
When your kitten has used the tray, scoop out the litter that was used. He won't use dirty litter. At the end of every day, clean and refill the tray.

Always wear rubber gloves

Remove used litter with the shovel

Accidents will happen!
All young kittens have accidents, so you must clean up the mess. Scrub the floor with water and disinfectant. Then spray it with odor remover. If your kitten can smell the mess, he will probably have another accident in the same spot.

Odor remover

Wear your gloves

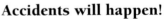

1 **To teach your cat how to use the cat-flap**, prop the flap open with a stick. He will discover that he can poke his head out to look around.

Use a small stick to lift up the flap

Cat climbs through the flap carefully

2 **Next, tempt your cat** through the flap door. Open the flap slightly and show him some food. He will nudge the flap open with his head, then climb through.

Hold out a bowl of food as a reward

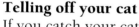

3 **Leave the cat-flap** unlocked during the day. Your cat will quickly learn how to use the flap without your help. He will soon come and go as he likes.

Cat darts out of flap

How to reward a good cat
🐾 Give him a big cuddle.
🐾 Play a game with him.
🐾 Give him a food treat.

Telling off your cat
If you catch your cat being naughty, say "No" sharply. Never hit him. If you do, he will think twice before coming near you again.

Point your finger at the naughty cat

Mischievous cat tries to eat plant

Fair punishment
You can scare your cat away from doing something naughty.

Spray your cat with a little water. He hates to be wet.

Loud noises frighten your cat.

Indoor cat

Cats spend a lot of time indoors. They like to find the warmest places to curl up and go to sleep, which won't always be in their beds. Your cat may not be able to go outside. But there are many different things that she can do indoors to keep active and fit.

A cardboard house is fun to hide in

Lookout platform

Swing the ball toy for your cat to swipe

Rough rope gives the cat a good grip for climbing

Adventure playground
You can make or buy an indoor activity center for your cat. It's a climbing frame, a scratching post, and a play area rolled into one. It should be sturdy, because cats hate walking on things that wobble.

Cat peeps out of tube

Fleece-lined tube makes a cozy, warm bed

Be ready to lift up the rope

Scratching post

Your cat needs to keep his claws trimmed. Buy a scratching post or make one out of rope. This should stop your cat from damaging furniture.

Cat rasps claws against carpet

Indoor games

Play "chase" games with your cat. Dangle a soft toy in front of her. Pull it away quickly when she tries to grab it. The cat will be much quicker than you.

Cardboard pyramid covered in carpet

Beware!

Cats may sleep in dangerous places.

Fuzzy cover keeps the cradle warm

Cat holds on to the toy with front paws

Keep the washing machine door shut.

Cat cradle

Your cat loves to lounge in a cradle hanging over a radiator. She will keep a lookout from this snug bed.

Make sure your cat can't climb into the car.

Your cat may prefer a bed without a roof

Keep a guard over the fireplace.

Cat curls up in basket

Time for bed

See where your cat most likes to sleep. Put his bed there. He will probably change his favorite place after a while.

Strange sleeping places

Sometimes you will find your cat sleeping in the most unlikely places. So keep on looking if you think he is lost!

Outdoor cat

Cats can go outside a week after they have had their inoculations (see p. 22). Your cat should stay in the yard, or he may be hurt in an accident. He practices hunting skills and marks out the area that belongs to him. He scratches and rubs against things to leave his scent. He makes regular patrols of his territory and may fight intruding cats (see p. 28).

Learning to hunt

Watch your cat creep up, wait for the right moment, and then pounce on leaves blowing in the wind. She is practicing her hunting skills.

Cat stalks rustling leaves

Paw ready to swipe

Cat creeps along fence

The athlete

Cats have an excellent sense of balance. They hardly ever fall from high places. They can run along very narrow ledges without fear of slipping. When cats jump, they crouch, and then spring into the air by suddenly straightening their strong back legs.

Front feet first

When cats jump down, they almost always land on their feet. The pads that are on their front paws cushion their landing.

Hind legs are tucked in

Front legs absorb shock

Cat stares down at you

Climbing high

Your cat likes to keep watch from the highest place he can climb to. He uses his hooked claws to climb up into trees. Cats either scramble or jump down.

A private place to go to the bathroom

Cats dig a hole where they want to go to the bathroom.

They squat over the hole. Most cats bury their droppings.

Cat sharpens his claws on bark

Beckoning will encourage your cat to come down if he is stuck

Scratching bark

A tree trunk makes a good scratching post for your cat. The fine scratch marks are messages. They tell other cats that the tree is in your cat's territory.

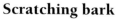

Cat stands up on back legs to scratch

Male cats may stand and spray urine to mark out their territory.

Cat's side rubs against plant to leave her smell

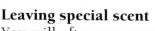

Leaving special scent

You will often see your cat rub her body against things in the yard to leave her unique scent. Other cats can tell from the scent whether your cat is male or female, and how long ago she was there.

Grooming your cat

Your cat is covered in fur from his nose to the tip of his tail. There are times when your cat sheds a lot of hair, called molting. He licks his coat regularly to make sure it stays clean, and to remove loose hairs. Groom your cat every day. This keeps his coat in good condition and helps him get used to being handled.

Paw is licked to wash face

Face washing

Your cat has a clever way of washing his face. He uses his saliva instead of soap and water, and his paw as a washcloth. He wipes his paw in circles around his cheeks. Then he reaches to wash behind his ears.

Head twists around to reach

Front teeth nibble away dirt

Removing bits of dirt

Dirt and tiny twigs get caught in your cat's fur. The fur also gets knotted. Your cat uses his small front teeth to pick out the dirt and untangle knots of hair.

❖ Fur balls

Your cat swallows the loose hair that he pulls out when he grooms himself. The fur usually passes straight out of him, but long-haired and molting cats may swallow too much fur. The hair sometimes rolls into a small ball in his stomach. If your cat coughs up fur balls, contact your veterinarian.

Back curves to let cat groom leg

Leg stretches up into the air

Rough tongue licks inside leg

Bending to lick all over

The surface of your cat's tongue is covered in hard little prongs. He uses it like a comb. His body is very flexible, so he can reach to groom almost every part of it.

Brushing a long-haired cat

Begin to groom your cat by brushing his back. Brush the coat from the head toward the tail. Your cat loves to feel the brush strokes on his back—he may even start to purr.

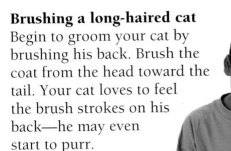

Cradle the cat in your lap

Happy cat starts to purr

Combing the hair

When you have brushed the coat, gently pull the comb through the hair. Don't be too rough. If you find a knot, untangle it with your fingers. Make sure you comb the whole coat, including the belly.

Comb one section of the coat at a time

Brushing short hair

Give your short-haired cat a quick brush all over every day. While you are brushing, you can check the condition of the coat (see p. 42).

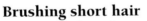

Brush the back first

Drying a wet cat

If your cat gets very wet, dry him with his own towel. Sit him between your knees and rub his coat all over. His paw pads may be muddy, so don't forget to wipe them.

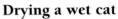

Wrap the towel around your cat

Your kitten grows up

You and your cat are a team for life. You will have to care for him every day of the year. When he is a kitten, you will have to care for him just like his mother did. By the time he is a year old, he will be grown up. He will do many things on his own but he will still like your company. Your cat will live a long time. When he is old, he will need special care.

Eye of very young kitten still closed

Caring for a kitten
A young kitten is helpless. He needs his mother to give him food and to clean up after him. His mother teaches him how to groom himself, hunt for food, and use a litter tray.

Playing games
When kittens are a few weeks old, they begin to play with one another. They learn all the skills they will need when they are older. By the time kittens are 14 weeks old, they are as agile and graceful as adult cats.

Kitten play-fights to practice his hunting skills

Rosette for the winning owner

Groomed coat

Prize-winning Ragdoll cat

Carefree as a kitten
A grown-up cat knows she can rely on you to give her food and a warm bed. She can spend time playing with you as she doesn't have to hunt for food.

Showing your cat
You can take your cat to a cat show. The judge will give prizes to the cats that are the best examples of their type, or breed. At other kinds of shows, your cat could win a prize for having the loudest purr or the bushiest tail!

Cat uses her tail to help her balance

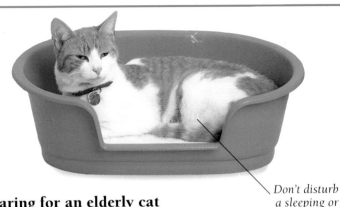

Caring for an elderly cat
When your cat is older, he will want to sleep more. He may find it difficult to reach to wash his coat, so he will need more help with grooming. Take him to the vet for regular check-ups.

Don't disturb a sleeping or resting old cat

Leaving your cat

Away from your pet
You can't always take your cat with you everywhere you go. You will have to leave him while you are at school, and when you go on vacation.

Out for a short time
Before you leave, make sure your pet has some food, fresh water, toys, and a clean litter tray. If you are happy to have your cat go outdoors, check that the cat-flap is unlocked.

Pet-sitting
When you go on vacation, your cat prefers to stay at home. Try to find a friend who is able to look after your pet every day. Write down a list of the daily jobs that need to be done, and the name and telephone number of your veterinarian.

The cattery
If no one can come to your home to care for your cat, you can put your pet in a cattery. This is like a hotel for cats. Whenever you travel with your cat, be sure to put him in a strong carrying basket.

Shake the rope so toy mice move

Paws grip toy mouse

Cat stands to reach toy

Neutering your kitten

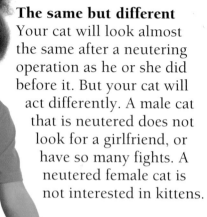

Just as women can have children, female cats can have kittens. There may be as many as eight kittens in a litter. You should think carefully about whether you want your cat to have kittens. Your veterinarian can give both female and male cats an operation that is called neutering. After it, your cat will not be able to have kittens.

☙ Responsible ownership

You may think it is fun for your female cat to have kittens. But it is best to have your cat neutered. Letting your cat have kittens can be very expensive. You need to do a lot of planning, and you have to find a good home for every one of the kittens.

The same but different
Your cat will look almost the same after a neutering operation as he or she did before it. But your cat will act differently. A male cat that is neutered does not look for a girlfriend, or have so many fights. A neutered female cat is not interested in kittens.

You won't see any difference

1 Newborn kittens can sleep, drink, and crawl. They suck their mother's nipples for milk. The mother cat spends a lot of time caring for her kittens. She licks them often to keep them clean.

Mother cat washes her baby

Mother stretches out leg to let kittens reach her nipples

Kitten jostles for a nipple

Eye is closed

Keen nose guides kitten to mother

2 **A four-day-old kitten** still cannot see or hear, but he has a strong sense of smell for finding his mother. He can crawl, but is very wobbly when he tries to stand up. By the time he is ten days old, his eyes will have opened and he will hear his first sounds.

3 **When a kitten is four weeks old**, he has learned to walk. He likes to play games with the other kittens in the litter and with his owner. In a few weeks time, he will be ready to leave his mother, and go to a new home.

Play with your kitten so he gets used to you

Tail raised for balance

Ear listens for the noise of the toy

Kitten has learned to walk on tiptoes

4 **At five months old**, a male kitten starts to be less playful. He is growing up quickly and may start to fight other cats. In a month's time, he and his sisters will be able to have kittens. It will be time to have them neutered.

Alert cat's ear is forward

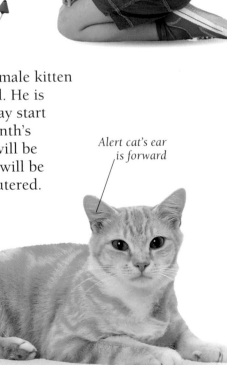

5 **After about a year**, your kitten will be a grown-up cat and is very independent. A male cat will patrol his territory regularly. If his sisters were not neutered, they could already have mothered a litter of kittens of their own.

Health care

You need to care for your cat properly to make sure that she stays fit and healthy. You should give her the right food (see p. 24), keep her well groomed (p. 36), and do several quick and simple health checks. If you do these every day, you will learn to quickly spot if your cat is unwell. If you think something is wrong, take her to your veterinarian as soon as possible.

Push fur backward

Healthy coat looks glossy

1 **Check that your cat's coat** is in good condition. Run your fingers through her fur. It should feel dry and smell clean. Do not forget to check hidden places, like under her tail.

Claw is the right length

Claw is too long

Use one arm to hold your cat around her middle

2 **Look carefully at your cat's paws.** Check that nothing is stuck in her pads or in the fur between her toes. Gently squeeze each paw so her claws come out. Make sure that they are clean and not too long.

Gently pull back the flap

3 **Examine your cat's ears.** Hold back the pointed part of each ear in turn and look down the hairy hole. The ear should be clean. If it smells, your cat may be ill.

4 Check your cat's eyes. A bright light will help you see them clearly. Put one hand under her chin, and the other on top of her head. Her eyes should be bright and shiny, with no tears in the corners.

Keep her head still

Your pet care checklist

Use this list to keep a record of all the jobs you need to do.

Copy this chart. Check off the jobs when you have finished them.

Every day:
Feed your cat
Clean bowls
Put down fresh water
Scoop out used litter
Groom coat
Check fur
Examine paws
Check ears and eyes
Look inside mouth
Clean teeth
Wash litter tray

◆

Once a week:
Weigh your cat
Tidy activity center
Check the food and litter supplies

◆

Once a month:
Give medicines
Wash blanket

◆

Every year:
Take your cat to the veterinarian for a check-up
Give cat inoculations

5 👭 Make sure nothing is stuck in your cat's mouth. Put one hand over her nose and tip her head back. Her mouth will start to open. Use your other hand to pull her jaw down. Her tongue should be pink.

Teeth should be clean and white

Pet toothpaste

Long-handled toothbrush

6 👭 Brush your cat's teeth every day. Put some pet toothpaste on your cat's toothbrush. Put the brush in the side of her mouth. Brush backward and forward along the outside of the teeth.

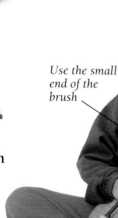

Use the small end of the brush

Hold your cat's jaw firmly

Visiting the veterinarian

The veterinarians and the veterinary assistants who work at your local vet's office want to keep your cat healthy and happy. They will tell you how to care for your cat properly. You can ask them as many questions as you like. They will also try to make your cat better if he is ill.

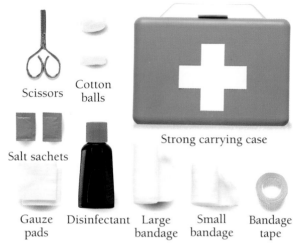

Scissors

Cotton balls

Strong carrying case

Salt sachets

Gauze pads

Disinfectant

Large bandage

Small bandage

Bandage tape

A first aid kit for cats

Prepare a special first aid kit for your cat. The veterinary assistant will explain how to use everything. Just like you, your cat sometimes cuts or grazes himself by accident. The kit contains all the things you need to make him feel better on the way to the vet's office.

Veterinary assistant holds cat for the veterinarian

A stethoscope is used to hear the cat's heartbeat

White coat keeps the vet clean

Your veterinary assistant

The veterinary assistant helps the veterinarian. She knows a lot about cats. If you have any questions about your cat, visit or telephone the veterinary assistant at your vet's office.

Your veterinarian

The veterinarian gives your cat special health checks. If your cat is ill, he will tell you what needs to be done to make him better. He may give you medicine for your cat.

My pet's fact sheet

Try making a fact sheet about your pet cat. Copy the headings on this page, or you can make up your own. Then write in the correct information about your cat.

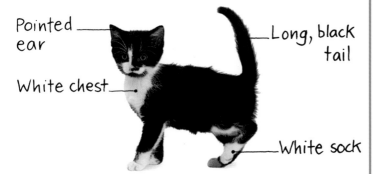

Pointed ear

Long, black tail

White chest

White sock

Leave a space to stick in a photograph or draw a picture of your cat. Then label all of your pet's special features.

Name: **Oreo**

Birthday: **August 21**

Weight: **2 pounds (900 grams)**

Type of food fed: **Dry food**

Best game: **Fish toy**

Veterinarian's name: **Mark Evans**

Veterinary assistant's name: **Thaddeus Weir**

Vet's office telephone number: **555-1234**

Medicines and injections

Your cat may be ill if tiny worms live inside him or insects crawl on his coat. To keep them away, the veterinary assistant will give you some special medicines for your cat. Germs can also make your cat sick. The veterinarian will give your cat inoculations every year to help protect him from them.

Index